IN WILDNESS . . .

The West of which I speak is but another name for the Wild, and what I have been preparing to say is, that in Wildness is the preservation of the World. Every tree sends its fibers forth in search of the Wild. The cities import it at any price. Men plow and sail for it. From the forest and wilderness come the tonics and barks which brace mankind. . . .

FROM Henry David Thoreau

"In Wildness Is the

INTRODUCTION BY Joseph Wood Krutch

Preservation of the World"

SELECTIONS & PHOTOGRAPHS BY

ELIOT PORTER

BALLANTINE BOOKS • NEW YORK

To Aline, who first suggested it

and

to Ellen, who taught me

detachment toward nature

this book is affectionately dedicated

The Walden quotations conform with the Riverside Press edition of 1894. The Journal
quotations, with one exception, conform with the *Journal* edition of 1906.
The first autumn page, dated November 1, 1853, conforms to the Riverside edition,
1892. The poem in the autumn section comes from *A Week on the Concord and
Merrimack Rivers*. The title comes from the essay entitled "Walking."
The passages from Thoreau's Journal are published through the courtesy of
Houghton Mifflin Co. The two opening lines of the Foreword are
from "The Tuft of Flowers," by Robert Frost, copyright 1934 by Holt, Rinehart
and Winston, Inc., copyright renewed 1962 by Robert Frost.
They are reprinted by permission of Holt, Rinehart and Winston, Inc.

The Sierra Club, founded in 1892 by John Muir, invites participation in its program—
a program that needs continuing and wide support—to preserve the nation's
scenic resources, including wilderness, wildlife, forests, and streams.

Addresses: 1050 Mills Tower, San Francisco, Calif. 94104

FOREWORD

Even to leaf through what has been created here is rewarding; but something quite wonderful happens to those who let themselves drift through. This is symbiotic art: Eliot Porter corroborates Thoreau and Thoreau verifies Porter, one never diminishing the other, for reasons Joseph Wood Krutch singles out as he tells how closely these men traveled together a century apart. Just as there is always something new to discover in Thoreau, there is much more than meets the eye in the photographs; a few impressions about the artist—the man who, ten years out of Harvard Medical School, gave up medicine and science for photography in 1939—may speed the discovery.

We ourselves discovered, or think we did, that the patience Dr. Porter acquired for bird photography has contributed enormously to the excellence of what he does here with inanimate subjects. He has learned to be alert to what a particular bird is likely to do in the next few minutes and to be ready when the bird meets his expectations. Having mastered the flightiness of such subjects, he could expect little trouble from the dependable peregrinations of sun, wind, and cloud.

The seasons performed just as dependably. Knowing a wild place well, Porter could anticipate what new life and form and color each change in the weather would reveal in that place, even as Thoreau had, and be there at the appointed hour. He would arrive fully sensitized and in sharp focus himself. Lens and image, we can see, responded unfailingly. If need be, abstractions would organize where only reality had been before. None but a very literal person would fail to see that color is his music, that there is melody line, counterpoint, harmony, dynamics, voicing, and phrasing all there for those who will listen.

There is absolute pitch, too—absolute color pitch. As we looked at the dye-transfer prints in Porter's exhibit, The Seasons, which the Smithsonian Institution circulates and from which the book derives, then peered at his four-by-five transparencies, and finally as we watched him review color proofs at the Barnes Press, we were quietly amazed by what this man knows about color. He remembers exactly what was there when the shutter let a moment's light in, and he knows what must happen technically if that moment is to be fixed. We have not yet seen all his colors in their natural habitat. But we are confident that if we borrow his acuity and walk out into waldens here and there, we shall find those colors ourselves. If we are very fortunate, once in a while they may perform for us the quiet symphony that responds to his baton.

Others, who are of unquestioned competence in these matters, must pass final judgment on Eliot Porter's greatness as a photographer. Some already have. I myself know only that I never saw color mean more than he makes it mean, and that I shall not easily overlook it again. The two Porter albums—the prints and the selections from Thoreau that were the manuscript for this book—made me vow openly to see it published even if I had to take up a life of crime to get the funds for it. Happily, Belvedere Scientific Fund intervened and provided generous assistance. It took responsible imagination to see as far beyond the mere beauty of the manuscript as needed seeing. Imaginative philanthropy followed.

To me it seems that much of what Henry David Thoreau wrote, more than a century ago, was less timely in his day than it is in ours: we can now prove that the natural and civilized worlds must live together or perish separately. We hope that the attitude of Thoreau and Porter toward unspoiled countryside will be pervasive. For there is no science and no art of greater importance than that which teaches seeing, which builds sensitivity and respect for the natural world, a world that "has visibly been recreated in the night." A natural world thus cherished will always bring "mornings when men are new-born, men who have the seeds of life in them."

DAVID BROWER

Berkeley, California
August 11, 1962

PREFACE

In a sense this book began when my father bought an island in Maine nearly half a century ago. Summer after summer its white beaches, its dense, spruce forests, its sour, salty, sea smells came back to life after the long gray winter. On Great Spruce Head Island among sweet fern and bunchberry, bay and twin flower, I found the tonic of wildness. In Maine I first read *Walden,* finding it rather a chore; in Maine I also became a photographer, and the subjects I photographed were things, I like to believe now, Thoreau might have described.

Shortly following World War II I became seriously involved with Thoreau's work. Just when this occurred and under what circumstances I no longer remember, but it was about this time that my wife suggested I do a book on Thoreau. My photographs, she thought, were like his writing. Her remark took deep root in my mind although I did little about it at first except to reread *Walden* and to collect Thoreau's works. Intermittently, in no logical order, I read them and slowly began to find out what kind of a person Thoreau had been and what he had said about the outdoors. At first I thought only the descriptive passages were suitable for a book of photographs, but on reading other authors, among whom Aldo Leopold and Joseph Wood Krutch influenced me most, those passages in which he wrote about man's relation to nature became greater in importance to the book I envisioned.

Fitting our time well and giving pause to our thoughts is Thoreau's admonition and despairing cry: "Most men, it seems to me, do not care for nature and would sell their share in all her beauty for a given sum. Thank God men have not yet learned to fly so they can lay waste the sky as well as the earth." Lines like these could not be illustrated, but they made me realize that illustration was not all I wanted to do. I hoped to be able to complement in feeling and spirit Thoreau's thinking one hundred years ago, and to show the peril we face even more today by our ever faster destruction of life not our own.

In the course of this time I was in Tucson one spring and with some hesitation went to Joseph Wood Krutch for advice on the book and to ask if he would write an introduction. To my surprise and delight he said he would. With this encouragement I went to work in earnest, selecting what I considered the best of Thoreau's writing, and photographing in all seasons the woods and streams and ponds and marshes in the northeastern states. Off and on for almost ten years this work continued until gradually text and photographs became part of one another. The time now seemed ripe to look for a publisher. I took it to several publishing houses and finally put it in the hands of an agent. It was rejected by all for the same reasons, their limited interest and its unlimited cost.

There was nothing I could do about the cost, but I could try to interest more people in the subject by making it more available. So I arranged an exhibition of prints and short quotations from Thoreau which I named "The Seasons." Following a first showing in Santa Fe, it went to Baltimore, Kansas City, and San Francisco; then the Smithsonian Institution asked for it as one of its traveling exhibitions. The first show under Smithsonian auspices was at George

Eastman House in Rochester, the opening of which I attended. While I was in Rochester Nancy Newhall introduced me by telephone to David Brower and suggested that the Sierra Club consider publishing the book. He asked to see it, was gratifyingly enthusiastic, and immediately set about obtaining the support necessary to make it a Sierra Club publication.

The title, a Thoreau quotation which the Wilderness Society has long used almost as a motto, was suggested by David Brower. Its eight words express the theme of the book and tell what Thoreau discovered one hundred years ago, that a leaven of wildness is necessary for the health of the human spirit, a truth we seem to have forgotten in our headlong rush to control all nature. Unless we reverse our course all wildness will disappear from the American continent even within the lives of those who are now the age Thoreau was when he died in 1862.

I wish to thank my wife Aline for her constant support, sympathy, and understanding during all the years that I worked on this book, Ellen Auerbach for her sensitive criticism and help with many of the pictures, Nancy Newhall for her work and encouragement in behalf of the book, Joseph Wood Krutch for his help and advice, directly and through his writings, in selecting many of the passages, and David Brower for his untiring devotion to highest publishing standards and to the purposes of the book.

ELIOT PORTER

Santa Fe, New Mexico
July 21, 1962

INTRODUCTION

Here, sensitively and with complete understanding, is presented through the medium of a new art that very world of American Nature which Thoreau, practicing one of the oldest of arts, taught us to see better than anyone ever had before. Eliot Porter makes no attempt merely to *document* the selected passages. To have done so would have been to produce no more than documentary illustrations. Instead—guided by sure artistic instinct—he has realized that the way to add to what Thoreau had written was to catch Thoreau's spirit, to see with his eye the kind of thing he saw and loved. As a result Porter's pictures are truly in the spirit of Thoreau.

What this means, first of all, is to discover how new and beautiful the familiar can be if we actually see it as though we had never seen it before. Other writers and other photographers are prone to seek out the unusual, the grandiose, and the far away. They shock us into awareness by flinging into our faces the obviously stupendous. When they are successful in their attempt they inspire in us that special sense of surprise, wonder, and a kind of pleasing terror which the eighteenth century defined as "awe." But the effect they produce is at the opposite pole from that aimed at and achieved by Thoreau.

John Muir is our great poet of the awesome aspects of the American scene. His subject matter complements that of Thoreau. But there could hardly be celebrants of nature more different. Thoreau's theme is not the remote and stupendous, but the daily and hourly miracle of the usually unnoticed beauty that is close at hand. He does not range the world seeking out the sensational. The chickadee and the violet are to him as striking as the flame tree or the bird of paradise. What we need is, he felt, not the unfamiliar but the power to realize that the familiar becomes unfamiliar once we really look at it, and that every aspect of the natural world is in its own way "awful."

One phase of the romantic revival of interest in nature was concerned especially with the "awesome" aspects. Byron illustrated this new interest when he wrote with a characteristically flamboyant rhetorical flourish his description of a thunderstorm in the Alps:

> And this was in the night, Most glorious night
> Thou wert not meant for slumber. Oh, let me be
> A sharer in thy fierce and far delight,
> A portion of the tempest and of thee.

Thoreau is far closer to Wordsworth and Wordsworth's even more familiar "The meanest flower that grows . . ." What one will find in Porter's pictures is the world of calm beauty at which one must look twice to find the awesomeness which is, nevertheless, there.

He with his camera—like Thoreau with his notebook and his "spyglass"—has "Traveled a good deal in Concord," and roundabout. The result is the very New England Thoreau saw more than one hundred years ago. Though the area still left to Nature has shrunk, what remains is what Thoreau saw, loved, and celebrated.

Even in his time he was aware that his beloved Concord had been more tamed than he would have liked to see it. "When I consider that the nobler animals have been exterminated here—the cougar, the panther, lynx, wolverine, wolf, bear, moose, the deer, the beaver, the turkey, etc., etc.—I cannot but feel as if I lived in a tame, and as it were, emasculated country. . . . I take infinite pains to know all the phenomena of spring, for instance, thinking that I have here the entire form, and then to my chagrin, I hear that it is but an imperfect copy that I possess and read, that my ancestors have torn out many of the first leaves and grandest passages, and mutilated it in many places." The process continues. Yet it may very well be that fewer animals and plants have actually disappeared completely since Thoreau's time than during the century that preceded him. It is the area left to them which has been most drastically curtailed. One must hunt longer to find what he found more readily. But as Porter's pictures show, most of the kind of thing he saw can still be seen.

How much longer that will be true is a question. Thoreau wondered that the village bell did not sound the knell when another tree was cut down. The trees continue to fall and any bell which is rung is less likely to be a knell than a celebration of Progress. "The squirrel has leaped to another tree, the hawk has circled further off, and is settled now upon a new eyrie, but the woodman is preparing to lay his axe at the root of that also."

So much for the subject matter of Porter's pictures. In what sense do their spirit and intention correspond to that of Thoreau?

Photography is the most modern but at the same time the least "modernistic" of the arts. Proponents of abstraction, surrealism, and the rest have long been accustomed to say that the camera has relieved the painter of a former function, namely, that of representation. Whether or not to be so relieved is actually a boon is still open to question. But there is no doubt about the fact that the photographer does deal in representations of the actual, whether it be the actuality of an external Nature or the actuality of a human portrait. Yet it is very far from true that he need be merely mechanical, that he can have no personal vision. He cannot, like the painter, impose upon Nature a pattern or design which isn't there. But he can select and frame his picture in such a way as to reveal the pattern and design which the merely casual observer has failed to see, either because he did not look closely enough or because it was confused by adjacent irrelevancies. The more the painter invents, the farther he takes us from the world which actually exists and to that extent he may even encourage us in an alienation from the real. The master photographer, on the other hand, discovers rather than invents, and in that way he may (as Porter so strikingly does) second Thoreau in Thoreau's most insistent injunction, namely, "Be not among those who have eyes that see not and ears that hear not."

It was no small task to select from the twenty volumes of Thoreau's published writings passages both so interesting in themselves and so susceptible to supplement and illumination by companion photographs as are those Porter has presented. Comparatively few of even those who profess an admiration for Thoreau's spirit have read one-tenth of what he left behind in the Journal from which he quarried his major published works, and from which he might have drawn several others. Many of his most brilliant passages of description and comment are buried in a text much of which became more pedestrian as the years went by. But Porter has ranged through the whole corpus and selected with so sure an insight those passages which are both remarkable in themselves and most suitable for his special undertaking that this volume is, among other things, one of the best anthologies ever compiled. His book is something to be read as well as looked at, and there is no student of his author so well versed that he will not get new insights from it.

Admirers of Walden and of the enormously rich Journal have found in them many different things: a theory of economics, a defense of nonconformity, a definition of the good life, and a defense of Thoreau's most persistent contention, namely, that human existence should be, not a duty or a burden, not a mere means to an end, but a self-justifying esthetic joy. Puritan in certain respects he was, but in this last mentioned attitude he was among the most defiant of antipuritans, as when he proclaimed that God had not sent him into this world without some spending money.

With none of these aspects of Thoreau's philosophy is Porter concerned, except perhaps by inference. What he does, however, illustrate so vividly is the conviction which underlies all the others, namely, the conviction that the source of the joy he sought, and of the wisdom he hoped to acquire, as well as the justification for his neglect of what others called the serious business of life, is the fact that "this curious world which we inhabit is more wonderful than it is convenient; more beautiful than it is useful; it is more to be admired and enjoyed than used."

Emanuel Kant propounded the theory that the magic of art depends in large part upon the various means which it uses to isolate the thing represented from all ordinary desires and duties in such a way that the only reaction possible to it is pure contemplation. We cannot pick the painted flower nor embrace the woman whom the artist has placed upon canvas. We can only look, see, and realize them. It was thus that Thoreau wished to contemplate rather than use Nature, and it is thus that we can enjoy Porter's photographs.

This is by no means to say that Thoreau was a mere esthete, one that is to whom natural beauty means only line, and shape, and color. In fact, some of the most heartfelt expressions of the scorn he was capable of is directed against those who, like the once popular English analyst of the picturesque William Gilpin, saw in Nature nothing except a picture. Gilpin talked, he said, "as if there were some food for the soul in mere light and shadow." He had, for example, undertaken to explain how a sleek well-fed horse might, no less than a shaggy one, be picturesque. "It is not his smooth and shining coat that makes him so. It is the apparent interruption of that smoothness by a variety of shades, and colors, which produces the effect." And Thoreau comments thus: "Not the slightest reference to the fact that this surface, with its lights and shades, belongs to a horse and not to a bag of wind. The same reasoning would apply equally well to one of his hind quarters hung bottom upwards in a butcher's stall. . . . I should say that no arrangement of light and shadow without reference to the object, actual or suggested, so lit and shaded can interest us powerfully, any more than paint itself can charm us." Gilpin had no fellow feeling, no sense of warmness.

Moreover, if Thoreau was no esthete, he was, if anything, still less a scientist—in the driest meaning of that term. It enraged him to buy a book on turtles and to find it nothing but anatomy. He did not, he protested, care to know the length of a hen hawk's intestines. And he had a deep sense of guilt when he once consented to send to Agassiz for pickling a specimen from his beloved Walden pond. If Nature was not a mere abstraction—as he feared it was to neighbor Emerson—neither was it something to be learned *about* rather than something to be learned from. On the one hand "it is not worthwhile to go around the world to count the cats in Zanzibar;" on the other, "a man has not seen a thing until he has felt it." One cannot even begin to "love Nature" in any profitable sense until one has achieved an empathy, a sense of oneness and of participation. "Appreciation" means an identification, a sort of mystical experience, religious in the most fundamental sense of the terms.

If the modern world is to learn from him what he has to teach, it must try to understand the what, why, and wherefore of the life he led and of his conviction that the only good life possible is one "natural" in a sense that society has tended more and more to corrupt. What, one must still ask, does it mean to observe Nature, to live with Nature, and to learn from it? How does one go about doing any of these things and what is it that one may hope to learn?

The two themes which reappear so persistently seem at first sight strangely disparate. On the one hand was Thoreau's search for what he called "wildness"; on the other, the search for the "higher laws" he never more than glimpsed but which he was sure Nature, even in her most savage aspects, was persistently whispering to him. The one search seems atavistic, the other transcendental, as though he were both going back to savagery and forward toward some higher mystical state. But the paradox is not unresolvable and in the resolution is the core of his faith.

Wildness, the merely natural and therefore almost animal life, is not sought for its own sake. Thoreau was no mere romantic admirer of the noble savage, and in Walden itself he makes this plain by examining the deficiencies of the best natural man he had ever known, namely the woodchopper. But the human race has lost its way. The road upward from the savage does not lead to the cluttered, materialistic, and desperate life such as that he sees his neighbors leading. To find the right road one must return in reality as well as in imagination to the origins. From them one might go forward again to a truly civilized, not a merely artificial, way of life.

Thoreau was aware that of his program he had achieved anything like full success only in what might be called its preliminary phases. He had simplified his life to the point where he had around it the wide margin which permitted him to live, rather than merely to make a living. He had made himself an inspector of snowstorms, and he had observed many natural phenomena. Certainly also he had achieved empathy—with both the wildness and the gentleness of Nature. Because of these successes he was sufficiently sure that he was on the right road confidently to advise others to take it. He had learned that it is not necessary to live by the sweat of one's brow unless "you sweat more easily than I do." He had found a happiness and contentment which were to him sure proof that his way of life was approved by whatever gods may be. But of the higher laws he admitted that he had caught only whispered hints. That chapter of Walden called "Higher Laws" merely reaffirms his sympathy with wildness along with his feeling that we have only begun to transcend it. No full revelation comes. But in the last chapter he can make the confident proclamation that "there is more day to dawn."

Just one hundred years ago Thoreau died. Before his death he shocked a pious relative who had asked if he had made his peace with God, by replying, "I am not aware that we ever quarreled." In the century which has passed since then no one has gone further than he along the road he chose and most have turned their backs even more irrevocably upon it. And whether or not this is the reason, the fact remains that the mass of men lead lives of a less and less quiet desperation. If those who believe in progress and define it as they do continue to have their way it will soon be impossible either to test his theory that Nature is the only proper context of human life or that in such a context we may ultimately learn the "higher laws."

One important function of a book like this will have been performed if it persuades those who open it that some remnant of the beauties it calls to our attention is worth preserving.

JOSEPH WOOD KRUTCH

Tucson, Arizona
June 14, 1962

SPRING

Remember thy creator in the days of thy youth. Rise free from care
before the dawn, and seek adventures. Let the noon find thee by other
lakes, and the night overtake thee everywhere at home. There are
no larger fields than these, no worthier games than may here be played.
Grow wild according to thy nature, like these sedges and brakes,
which will never become English hay. Let the thunder rumble; what if it
threaten ruin to farmers' crops? That is not its errand to thee.
Take shelter under the cloud, while they flee to carts and sheds. Let not to
get a living be thy trade, but thy sport. Enjoy the land, but own it not.
Through want of enterprize and faith men are where they are, buying
and selling, and spending their lives like serfs. — *Walden*

February 12, 1860

At a distance in several directions I see the tawny earth streaked or
spotted with white where the bank or hills and fields appear, or else the
green-black evergreen forests, or the brown, or russet, or tawny deciduous
woods, and here and there, where the agitated surface of the river is
exposed, the blue-black water. That dark-eyed water, especially where
I see it at right angles with the direction of the sun, is it not the first sign
of spring? How its darkness contrasts with the general lightness of the
winter! It has more life in it than any part of the earth's surface.
It is where one of the arteries of the earth is palpable, visible.

March 8, 1840

In the brooks the slight grating sound of small cakes of ice,
floating with various speed, is full of content and promise, and where the
water gurgles under a natural bridge, you may hear these hasty rafts
hold conversation in an undertone. Every rill is a channel for the juices
of the meadow. Last year's grasses and flower-stalks have been steeped
in rain and snow, and now the brooks flow with meadow tea. . . .

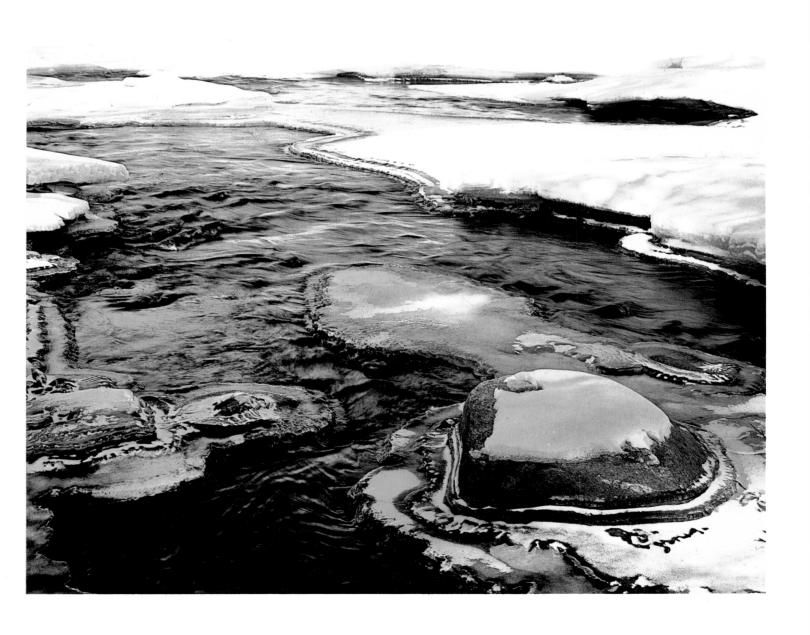

These earliest spring days are peculiarly pleasant. We shall have
no more of them for a year. I am apt to forget that we may have raw and
blustering days a month hence. The combination of this delicious air,
which you do not want to be warmer or softer, with the presence
of ice and snow, you sitting on the bare russet portions, the south
hillsides, of the earth, this is the charm of these days. It is the
summer beginning to show itself like an old friend in the midst of winter.
You ramble from one drier russet patch to another. These are
your stages. You have the air and sun of summer, over snow
and ice, and in some places even the rustling of dry leaves
under your feet, as in Indian-summer days.

March 30, 1840

Pray, what things interest me at present? A long, soaking rain,
the drops trickling down the stubble, while I lay drenched on last year's
bed of wild oats, by the side of some bare hill, ruminating.
These things are of moment. To watch this crystal globe just sent
from heaven to associate with me. While these clouds and this sombre
drizzling weather shut all in, we two draw nearer and know one another.
The gathering in of the clouds with the last rush and dying breath
of the wind, and then the regular dripping of twigs and leaves the country
o'er, the impression of inward comfort and sociableness, the drenched
stubble and trees that drop beads on you as you pass, their dim outline
seen through the rain on all sides dropping in sympathy with yourself.
These are my undisputed territory. This is Nature's English comfort. The
birds draw closer and are more familiar under the thick foliage,
composing new strains on their roosts against the sunshine.

March 10, 1859

I perceive the spring in the softened air . . . Looking through
this transparent vapor, all surfaces, not osiers and open water alone,
look more vivid. The hardness of winter is relaxed.
There is a fine effluence surrounding the wood, as if the sap had begun
to stir and you could detect it a mile off. Such is the difference
between an object seen through a warm, moist, and soft air and a cold,
dry, hard one. Such is the genialness of nature that the trees appear to have
put out feelers by which the senses apprehend them more tenderly.
I do not know that the woods are ever more beautiful, or affect me more.

March 17, 1859

When I am opposite the end of the willow-row, seeing the osiers of
perhaps two years old all in a mess, they are seen to be very distinctly
yellowish beneath and scarlet above. They are fifty rods off.
Here is the same chemistry that colors the leaf or fruit, coloring the bark.
It is generally, perhaps always, the upper part of the twig, the more
recent growth, that is the higher-colored and more flower or fruit like.
So leaves are more ethereal the higher up and farther from the root.
In the bark of the twigs, indeed, is the more permanent flower
or fruit. The flower falls in spring or summer, the fruit and leaves fall or
wither in autumn, but the blushing twigs retain their color
throughout the winter and appear more brilliant than ever
the succeeding spring. They are winter fruit.

March 30, 1856

How silent are the footsteps of spring! There, too, where there is a
fraction of the meadow, two rods over, quite bare, under the bank, in this
warm recess at the head of the meadow, though the rest of the meadow
is covered with snow a foot or more in depth, I was surprised to see
the skunk-cabbage, with its great spear-heads open and ready to blossom . . .
The spring advances in spite of snow and ice, and cold even.

December 24, 1841

I want to go soon and live away by the pond, where I shall hear only
the wind whispering among the reeds. It will be success if I shall have left
myself behind. But my friends ask what I will do when I get there.
Will it not be employment enough to watch the progress of the seasons?

For the first week, whenever I look out on the pond it impressed me like
a tarn high up on the side of a mountain, its bottom far above the surface
of other lakes, and, as the sun rose, I saw it throwing off its nightly
clothing of mist, and here and there, by degrees, its soft ripples or its
smooth reflecting surface was revealed, while the mists, like ghosts, were
stealthily withdrawing in every direction into the woods, as at the
breaking up of some nocturnal conventicle. The very dew seemed to hang
upon the trees later into the day than usual, as on the sides of mountains.

— *Walden*

April 9, 1859

We sit by the side of little Goose Pond . . . to watch the ripples on it.
Now it is merely smooth, and then there drops down on to it, deep as it
lies amid the hills, a sharp and narrow blast of the icy north wind
careening above, striking it, perhaps, by a point or an edge,
and swiftly spreading along it, making a dark-blue ripple. Now four or
five windy bolts, sharp or blunt, strike it at once and spread
different ways. The boisterous but playful north wind evidently stoops
from a considerable height to dally with this fair pool which it discerns
beneath. You could sit there and watch these blue shadows playing
over the surface like the light and shade on changeable silk, for hours.
It reminds me, too, of the swift Camilla on a field [of] grain.
The wind often touches the water only by the finest points or edges.
It is thus when you look in some measure from the sun, but if you move
around so as to come more opposite to him, then these dark-blue
ripples are all sparkles too bright to look at, for now you see
the sides of the wavelets which reflect the sun to you.

March 28, 1859

How charming the contrast of land and water, especially a
temporary island in the flood, with its new and tender shores of waving
outline, so withdrawn yet habitable, above all if it rises into a hill
high above the water and contrasting with it the more, and
if that hill is wooded, suggesting wilderness! Our vernal lakes have a
beauty to my mind which they would not possess if they were
more permanent. Everything is in rapid flux here, suggesting that
Nature is alive to her extremities and superficies.

March 10, 1853

This is the first really spring day . . . Something analogous to the
thawing of the ice seems to have taken place in the air. At the end of
winter there is a season in which we are daily expecting spring,
and finally a day when it arrives . . . Methinks the first obvious evidence
of spring is the pushing out of the swamp willow catkins . . . then the
pushing up of skunk-cabbage spathes (and pads at the bottom of water).

October 25, 1857

She appears, and we are once more children; we commence again
our course with the new year.

March 18, 1858

Each new year is a surprise to us. We find that we had virtually
forgotten the note of each bird, and when we hear it again it is
remembered like a dream, reminding us of a previous state of existence.
How happens it that the associations it awakens are always
pleasing, never saddening; reminiscenses of our sanest hours?
The voice of nature is always encouraging.

June 2, 1858

Probably these crests of the earth are for the most part of one color
in all lands, that gray color . . . which nature loves; color of unpainted
wood, weather-stain, time-stain; not glaring nor gaudy; the color of all
roofs, the color of all things that endure, the color that wears well; color
of Egyptians ruins, of mummies and all antiquity: baked in the sun,
done brown . . . not scarlet, like the crest of the bragging cock, but that
hard, enduring gray; a terrene sky-color; solidified air with a tinge of earth.

March 13, 1842

Nature doth thus kindly heal every wound. By the mediation of a
thousand little mosses and fungi, the most unsightly objects become
radiant of beauty. There seem to be two sides of this world, presented us
at different times, as we see things in growth or dissolution, in life
or death. For seen with the eye of the poet, as God sees them, all things
are alive and beautiful; but seen with the historical eye, or eye of the
memory, they are dead and offensive. If we see Nature as pausing,
immediately all mortifies and decays; but seen as progressing, she is beautiful.

May 23, 1853

How different the ramrod jingle of the chewink or any bird's note
sounds now at 5 P.M. in the cooler, stiller air, when also the humming of
insects is more distinctly heard, and perchance some impurity has
begun to sink to earth strained by the air! Or is it, perchance,
to be referred to the cooler, more clarified and pensive state of the mind,
when dews have begun to descend in it and clarify it? Chaste eve!
A certain lateness in the sound, pleasing to hear, which releases me
from the obligation to return in any particular season. I have passed the
Rubicon of staying out. I have said to myself, that way is not homeward;
I will wander further from what I have called my home — to the
home which is forever inviting me. In such an hour the freedom
of the woods is offered me, and the birds sing my dispensation.
In dreams the links of life are united: we forget that
our friends are dead; we know them as of old.

March 18, 1858

But, ah! the needles of the pine, how they shine, as I look down
over the Holden wood and westward! Every tree is lit with the most
subdued, but clear ethereal light, as if it were the most delicate frost work
in a winter morning, reflecting no heat, but only light.
And as they rock and wave in the strong wind, even a mile off,
the light courses up and down there as over a field of grain; . . . like
looms above the forest, when the shuttle is thrown between
the light woof and the dark web. . . .

February 25, 1860

I noticed yesterday the first conspicuous silvery sheen from the needles
of the white pine waving in the wind. A small one was conspicuous by the
side of the road. . . . I suspect that those plumes which
have been oppressed or contracted by snow and ice are not only dried
but opened and spread by the wind.

March 10, 1852

I was reminded, this morning before I rose, of those undescribed
ambrosial mornings of summer which I can remember, when a thousand
birds were heard gently twittering and ushering in the light, like the
argument to a new canto of an epic and heroic poem. The serenity, the
infinite promise, of such a morning! The song or twitter of birds
drips from the leaves like dew. Then there was something divine and
immortal in our life, when I have waked up on my couch in the woods
and seen the day dawning, and heard the twittering of the birds.

Early in May, the oaks, hickories, maples, and other trees,
just putting out amidst the pine woods around the pond, imparted a
brightness like sunshine to the landscape, especially in cloudy
days, as if the sun were breaking through mists and shining
faintly on the hill-sides here and there. — *Walden*

June 1, 1854

Within a little more than a fortnight the woods, from bare twigs,
have become a sea of verdure, and young shoots have contended with one
another in the race. The leaves are unfurled all over the country. . . .
Shade is produced, and the birds are concealed and their economies go
forward uninterruptedly, and a covert is afforded to animals
generally. But thousands of worms and insects are preying on the leaves
while they are young and tender. Myriads of little parasols are suddenly
spread all the country over, to shield the earth and the roots of the trees
from the parching heat, and they begin to flutter and rustle in the breeze.

It is impossible to remember a week ago. A river of Lethe flows
with many windings the year through, separating one season from another.
The heavens for a few days have been lost. It has been a sort of
paradise instead. As with the seashore, so it is with the universal
earth-shore, not in summer can you look far into the ocean
of the ether. They who come to this world as to a watering-place in the
summer for coolness and luxury never get the far and fine
November views of heaven. Is not all the summer akin to a paradise?
We have to bathe in ponds to brace ourselves. The earth is
blue now, — the near hills, in this haze.

September 28, 1852

Ah, if I could put into words that music which I hear; that music which can bring tears to the eyes of marble statues! — to which the very muscles of men are obedient!

May 17, 1854

The splendid rhodora now sets the swamps on fire with its masses
of rich color. It is *one of the first* flowers to catch the eye at a distance in
masses, — so naked, unconcealed by its own leaves.

May 23, 1854

We soon get through with Nature. She excites an expectation which
she cannot satisfy. The merest child which has rambled into a copsewood
dreams of a wildness so wild and strange and inexhaustible as
Nature can never show him. . . . There was a time when the beauty and
the music were all within, and I sat and listened to my thoughts,
and there was a song in them. I sat for hours on rocks and wrestled with
the melody which possessed me. I sat and listened by the hour to a
positive though faint and distant music, not sung by any bird,
nor vibrating any earthly harp. When you walked with a joy which knew
not its own origin. When you were an organ of which the world
was but one poor broken pipe. I lay long on the rocks,
foundered like a harp on the seashore, that knows not how it is
dealt with. You sat on the earth as on a raft, listening to music that was
not of the earth, but which ruled and arranged it. Man *should be*
the harp articulate. When you cords were tense.

March 22, 1861

When we consider how soon some plants which spread rapidly,
by seeds or roots, would cover an area equal to the surface of the globe,
. . . how soon some fishes would fill the ocean if all their ova
became full-grown fishes, we are tempted to say that every organism,
whether animal or vegetable, is contending for the possession of the
planet. . . . Nature opposes to this many obstacles, as climate, myriads of
brute and also human foes, and of competitors which may preoccupy
the ground. Each suggests an immense and wonderful greediness
and tenacity of life . . . as if bent on taking entire possession of the globe
wherever the climate and soil will permit. And each prevails
as much as it does, because of the ample preparations it has made
for the contest, — it has secured a myriad chances, — because
it never depends on spontaneous generation to save it.

March 23, 1856

I seek acquaintance with Nature, — to know her moods and manners.
Primitive nature is the most interesting to me. I take infinite pains to
know all the phenomena of spring, for instance, thinking that I have here
the entire poem, and then, to my chagrin, I learn that it is but
an imperfect copy that I possess and have read, that my ancestors have
torn out many of the first leaves and grandest passages, and mutilated it
in many places. I should not like to think that some demigod
had come before me and picked out some of the best of the stars.
I wish to know an entire heaven and an entire earth.

SUMMER

We need the tonic of wildness, to wade sometimes in marshes where
the bittern and the meadow-hen lurk, and hear the booming of the snipe;
to smell the whispering sedge where only some wilder and more
solitary fowl builds her nest, and the mink crawls with its belly close
to the ground. At the same time that we are earnest to explore
and learn all things, we require that all things be mysterious and
unexplorable, that land and sea be infinitely wild, unsurveyed
and unfathomed by us because unfathomable. We can never have enough
of nature. We must be refreshed by the sight of inexhaustible vigor,
vast and titanic features, the sea-coast with its wrecks, the
wilderness with its living and its decaying trees, the thunder cloud,
and the rain which lasts three weeks and produces freshets.
We need to witness our own limits transgressed, and some life
pasturing freely where we never wander. — *Walden*

June 6, 1856

How well suited the lining of a bird's nest, not only for the
comfort of the young, but to keep the eggs from breaking! Fine elastic
grass stems or root fibers, pine needles, or hair, or the like.
These tender and brittle things which you can hardly carry
in cotton lie there without harm.

June 6, 1857

This is June, the month of grass and leaves. . . . Already the aspens are
trembling again, and a new summer is offered me. I feel a little fluttered in
my thoughts, as if I might be too late. Each season is but an
infinitesimal point. It no sooner comes than it is gone. It has no duration.
It simply gives a tone and hue to my thought. Each annual phenomenon
is a reminiscence and prompting. Our thoughts and sentiments answer
to the revolutions of the seasons, as two cog-wheels fit into each other.
We are conversant with only one point of contact at a time, from
which we receive a prompting and impulse and instantly pass
to a new season or point of contact. A year is made up of a certain series
and number of sensations and thoughts which have their language
in nature. Now I am ice, now I am sorrel. Each experience
reduces itself to a mood of the mind.

June 11, 1852

As I climbed the Cliffs, when I jarred the foliage, I perceived an exquisite
perfume which I could not trace to its source. Ah, those fugacious
universal fragrances of the meadows and woods! odors rightly mingled!

June 14, 1851

Where my path crosses the brook in the meadow there is a singularly
sweet scent in the heavy air . . . where the brakes grow, — the fragrance of
the earth, as if the dew were a distillation of the fragrant essences of
Nature. . . . And now my senses are captivated again by a sweet
fragrance as I enter the embowered willow causeway, and I know not if
it be from a particular plant or all together, —
sweet-scented vernal grass or sweet-brier.

June 9, 1850

Who taught the oven-bird to conceal her nest? It is on the ground,
yet out of sight. What cunning there is in nature! No man could have
arranged it more artfully for the purpose of concealment.
Only the escape of the bird betrays it.

July 3, 1853

The Oven-bird's nest in Laurel Glen is near the edge of an open pine
wood, under a fallen pine twig and a heap of dry oak leaves.
Within these, on the ground, is the nest, with a dome-like top
and an arched entrance of the whole height and width on one side.
Lined within with dry pine needles.

June 7, 1853

The oven-bird runs from her covered nest, so close to the ground
under the lowest twigs and leaves, even the loose leaves on the ground,
like a mouse, that I cannot get a fair view of her. She does not fly at all.
Is it to attract me, or partly to protect herself?

June 26, 1852

And the water-lily floats on the smooth surface of slow waters, amid
rounded shields of leaves, bucklers, red beneath, which simulate a green
field, perfuming the air. Each instantly the prey of the spoiler, —
the rose-bug and water-insects. How transitory the perfect beauty of the
rose and the lily! The highest, intensest color belongs to the land,
the purest, perchance, to the water. The lily is perhaps the
only flower which all are eager to pluck. . . .

June 20, 1853

Found two lilies open in the very shallow inlet of the meadow.
Exquisitely beautiful, and unlike anything else that we have, is the first
white lily just expanded in some shallow lagoon where the water is
leaving it, — perfectly fresh and pure, before the insects have discovered it.
How admirable its purity! How innocently sweet its fragrance!
How significant that the rich, black mud of our dead stream
produces the water-lily, — out of that fertile slime springs this spotless
purity! It is remarkable that those flowers which are most
emblematical of purity should grow in the mud.

July 4, 1860

Standing on J. P. Brown's land, south side, I observed his rich and
luxuriant uncut grass-lands northward, now waving under the easterly
wind. It is a beautiful camilla, sweeping like waves of light and shade over
the whole breadth of his land, like a low steam curling over it,
imparting wonderful life to the landscape, like the light and shade of a
changeable garment. . . . It is an interesting feature, very easily overlooked,
and suggests that we are wading and navigating at present in a sort of
sea of grass, which yields and undulates under the wind like water; and so,
perchance, the forest is seen to do from a favorable position.
Early, there was that flashing light of waving pine in the horizon;
now, the Camilla on grass and grain.

June 30, 1840

In this fresh evening each blade and leaf looks as if it had been
dipped in an icy liquid greenness.

June 4, 1854

Now is the time [to] observe the leaves, so fair in color and so perfect
on form. I stood over a sprig of choke-cherry, with fair and perfect glossy
green obovate and serrate leaves, in the woods this P.M., as if it were
a rare flower. Now the various forms of oak leaves in the sprout-lands,
wet-glossy, as if newly painted green and varnished, attract me.
The chinquapin and black shrub oaks are such leaves as I fancy crowns
were made of. And in the washing breeze the lighter undersides
begin to show, and a new light is flashed upon the year,
lighting up and enlivening the landscape.

June 22, 1853

As I come over the hill, I hear the wood thrush singing his evening lay.
This is the only bird whose note affects me like music, affects the flow
and tenor of my thoughts, my fancy and imagination. It lifts and
exhilerates me. . . . It is a medicative draught to my soul.
It is an elixir to my eyes and a fountain of youth to all my senses.
It changes all hours to an eternal morning. It banishes all trivialness.
It reinstates me in my dominion, makes me the lord of creation, is chief
musician of my court. This minstrel sings in a time, a heroic age, with
which no event in the village can be contemporary. How can they be
contemporary when only the latter is *temporary* at all? . . . So there is
something in the music of the cow-bell, something sweeter and
more nutritious, than in the milk which the farmers drink. This thrush's
song is a *ranz des vaches* to me. I long for wildness, a nature which
I cannot put my foot through, woods where the woodthrush forever sings,
where the hours are early morning ones, and there is dew on the grass,
and the day is forever unproved, where I might have a fertile
unknown for a soil about me. I would go after the cows,
I would watch the flocks of Admetus there forever, only for my board
and clothes, a New Hampshire everlasting and unfallen. . . .
All that was ripest and fairest in the wildness and the wild man is
preserved and transmitted to us in the strain of the wood thrush. It is the
mediator between barbarism and civilization. It is unrepentant as Greece.

June 27, 1859

I find an *Attacus luna* half hidden under a skunk-cabbage leaf,
with its back to the ground and motionless, on the edge of a swamp.
The under side is a particularly pale hoary green. It is somewhat greener
above with a slightly purplish brown border on the front edge of its
front wings, and a brown, yellow, and whitish eye-spot in the middle of
each wing. It is very sluggish and allows me to turn it over
and cover it up with another leaf, — sleeping till the night comes.
It has more relation to the moon by its pale hoary-green color and its
sluggishness by day than by the form of its tail.

June 23, 1852

It seems natural that rocks which have lain under the heavens so long should be gray, as it were an intermediate color between the heavens and the earth. The air is the thin paint in which they have been dipped and brushed with the wind. Water, which is more fluid and like the sky in its nature, is still more like it in color. Time will make the most discordant materials harmonize. . . .

June 17, 1854

A cold fog. These mornings those who walk in grass are thoroughly
wetted above mid-leg. All the earth is dripping wet. I am surprised to feel
how warm the water is, by contrast with the cold, foggy air. . . .
The dewy cobwebs are very thick this morning, little napkins
of the fairies spread on the grass.

July 7, 1852

There is everywhere dew on the cobwebs, little gossamer veils
or scarfs as big as your hand, dropped from the fairy shoulders that
danced on the grass the past night.

November 9, 1857

Mr. Farmer tells me that one Sunday he went to his barn, having
nothing to do, and thought he would watch the swallows, republican
swallows. The old bird was feeding her young, and he sat within
fifteen feet, overlooking them. There were five young, and he was curious
to know how each received its share; and as often as the bird came
with a fly, the one at the door (or opening) took it, and then they all
hitched round one notch, so that a new one was presented at the door,
who received the next fly; and this was the invariable order, the
same one never received two flies in succession. At last the old bird
brought a very small fly, and the young one that swallowed it did not
desert his ground but waited to receive the next, but when
the bird came with another, of the usual size, she commenced a loud
and long scolding at the little one, till it resigned its place,
and the next in succession received the fly.

The large buds, suddenly pushing out late in the spring from dry sticks
which had seemed to be dead, developed themselves as by magic
into graceful green and tender boughs, an inch in diameter; and sometimes
as I sat at my window, so heedlessly did they grow and tax their
weak joints, I heard a fresh and tender bough suddenly fall like a fan to
the ground, when there was not a breath of air stirring, broken off
by its own weight. In August, the large masses of berries, which,
when in flower, had attracted many wild bees, gradually assumed
their bright velvety crimson hue, and by their weight again
bent down and broke the tender limbs. — *Walden*

October 26, 1853

I well remember the time this year when I first heard the dream of
the toads. I was laying out house-lots on Little River in Haverhill.
We had had some raw, cold and wet weather. But this day was remarkably
warm and pleasant, and I had thrown off my outside coat. I was going
home to dinner, past a shallow pool, which was green with springing
grass, . . . when it occurred to me that I heard the dream of the toad.
It rang through and filled all the air, though I had not heard it once.
And I turned my companion's attention to it, but he did not appear to
perceive it as a new sound in the air. Loud and prevailing as it is,
most men do not notice it at all. It is to them, perchance, a sort of
simmering or seething of all nature. That afternoon the dream
of the toads rang through the elms by Little River and affected the
thoughts of men, though they were not conscious that they heard it.
How watchful we must be to keep the crystal well that we are made, clear!

June 17, 1854

It is dry, hazy June weather. We are more of the earth, farther from
heaven these days. We live in a grosser element. We [are] getting deeper
into the mists of earth. Even the birds sing with less vigor and
vivacity. The season of hope and promise is past; already the season
of small fruits has arrived. The Indian marked the midsummer as the
season when berries were ripe. We are a little saddened,
because we begin to see the interval between our hopes and their
fulfillment. The prospect of the heavens is taken way,
and we are presented only with a few small berries.

Sitting on the Conantum house sill (still left), I see two and perhaps three young striped squirrels, two-thirds grown, within fifteen or twenty feet, one or more on the wall and another on the ground.

Their tails are rather imperfect, as their bodies. They are running about, yet rather feebly, nibbling the grass, etc., or sitting upright, looking very cunning. The broad white line above and below the eye make it look very long as well as large, and the black and white stripe on its sides, curved as it sits, are very conspicuous and pretty. Who striped the squirrel's side? Several times I saw two approach each other and playfully and, as it were, affectionatly put their paws and noses to each other's faces. Yet this was done very deliberately and affectionately. There was no rudeness nor excessive activity in the sport. At length the old one appears, larger and much more bluish, and shy, and, with a sharp cluck or chip, calls the others gradually to her and draws them off along the wall, they from time to time frisking ahead of her, then she ahead of them. The hawks must get many of these inexperienced creatures.

AUTUMN

November 1, 1853

Few come to the woods to see how the pine lives and grows and spires,
lifting its evergreen arms to the light, to see its perfect success.
Most are content to behold it in the shape of many broad boards brought
to market, and deem that its true success. The pine is no more lumber
than man is, and to be made into boards and houses is no more its
true and highest use than the truest use of man is to be cut down and
made into manure. A pine cut down, a dead pine, is no more a pine than
a dead human carcass is a man. Is it the lumberman who is the friend
and lover of the pine, stands nearest to it, and understands its nature best?
Is it the tanner or turpentine distiller who posterity will fable was
changed into a pine at last? No, no, it is the poet who makes the truest
use of the pine, who does not fondle it with an axe, or tickle it with a
saw, or stroke it with a plane. It is the poet who loves it as his own
shadow in the air, and lets it stand. It is as immortal as I am,
and will go to as high a heaven, there to tower above me still. Can he who
has only discovered the value of whale-bone and whale-oil be said to
have discovered the true uses of the whale? Can he who slays the elephant
for his ivory be said to have seen the elephant? No, these are petty and
accidental uses. Just as if a stronger race were to kill us in order
to make buttons and flageolets of our bones, and then prate of the
usefulness of man. Every creature is better alive than dead, both men and
moose and pine-trees, as life is more beautiful than death.

Flint's Pond! Such is the poverty of our nomenclature. What right
had the unclean and stupid farmer, whose farm abutted on this sky water,
whose shores he had ruthlessly laid bare, to give his name to it?
Some skin-flint, who loved better the reflecting surface of a dollar, or a
bright cent, in which he could see his own brazen face; who
regarded even the wild ducks which settled in it as trespassers; his fingers
grown into crooked and horny talons from the long habit of
grasping harpy-like; — so it is not named for me. I go not there to see him
nor to hear of him; who never *saw* it, who never bathed in it,
who never loved it, who never protected it, who never spoke a good
word for it, nor thanked God that He made had it. Rather let it be
named from the fishes that swim in it, the wild fowl or quadrupeds which
frequent it, the wild flowers which grow by its shores, or some wild
man or child the thread of whose history is interwoven with its own; not
from him who could show no title to it but the deed which a
like-minded neighbor or legislature gave him, — him who thought only
of its money value; whose present perchance cursed all the shore;
who exhausted the land around it, and would fain have exhausted the
waters within it; who regretted only that it was not English hay or
cranberry meadow, — there was nothing to redeem it, forsooth, in his
eyes, — and would have drained and sold it for the mud at its bottom.
It did not turn his mill, and it was no privilege to him to behold it. I
respect not his labors, his farm where everything has its price, who would
carry the landscape, who would carry his God, to market, if he could get
anything for him; who goes to market *for* his god as it is; on whose
farm nothing grows free, whose fields bear no crops, whose meadows no
flowers, whose trees no fruit, but dollars; who loves not the beauty
of his fruits, whose fruits are not ripe for him till they are turned to
dollars. Give me the poverty that enjoys true wealth. — *Walden*

September 26, 1854

Some single red maples are very splendid now, the whole tree
bright-scarlet against the cold green pines; now when very few trees are
changed, a most remarkable object in the landscape; seen a mile off.
It is too fair to be believed, especially seen against the light. Some are
a reddish or else greenish yellow, others with red or yellow cheeks.
I suspect that the yellow maples had not scarlet blossoms.

October 24, 1858

The brilliant autumnal colors are red and yellow and the various tints,
hues, and shades of these. Blue is reserved to be the color of the sky, but
yellow and red are the colors of the earth-flower. Every fruit,
on ripening, and just before its fall, acquires a bright tint. So do the
leaves; so the sky before the end of the day, and the year near its setting.
October is the red sunset sky, November the later twilight. Color
stands for all ripeness and success. We have dreamed that the hero should
carry his color aloft, as a symbol of the ripeness of his virtue. The
noblest feature, the eye, is the fairest-colored, the jewel of the body.

October 9, 1857

It has come to this, — that the lover of art is one, and the lover of
nature another, though true art is but the expression of our love of nature.
It is monstrous when one cares but little about trees and much
about Corinthian columns, and yet this is exceedingly common.

November 13, 1858

It is wonderful what gradation and harmony there is in nature.
The light reflected from bare twigs at this season — i.e., since they began
to be bare, in the latter part of October — is not only like that from
gossamer, but like that which will ere long be reflected from the
ice that will incrust them. So the bleached herbage of the fields is like
frost, and frost like snow, and one prepares for the other.

October 24, 1837

Every part of nature teaches that the passing away of one life
is the making room for another. The oak dies down to the ground,
leaving within its rind a rich virgin mould, which will impart a vigorous
life to an infant forest. The pine leaves a sandy and sterile soil,
the harder woods a strong and fruitful mould.
So this constant abrasion and decay makes the soil of our future growth.
As I live now so shall I reap. If I grow pines and birches,
my virgin mould will not sustain the oak; but pines and birches, or,
perchance, weeds and brambles, will constitute my second growth.

Time is but the stream I go a-fishing in. I drink at it; but while I drink
I see the sandy bottom and detect how shallow it is. Its thin current slides
away, but eternity remains. I would drink deeper; fish in the sky,
whose bottom is pebbly with stars. I cannot count one. I know not the
first letter of the alphabet. I have always been regretting
that I was not as wise as the day I was born. — *Walden*

September 27, 1857

. . . blackberry vines here and there in sunny places look like
a streak of blood on the grass.

October 2, 1857

Sitting on a rock east of Trillium Woods, I perceive that,
generally speaking, it is only the lower edge or *pediment* of the woods
that shows the bright autumnal tints yet, the birches, very young oaks and
hickories, huckleberry bushes, blackberries, etc., that stand around
the edges, though here and there some taller maple flames upward amid
the masses of green, or some other riper and mellower tree.

October 3, 1858

Standing on the railroad I look across the pond to Pine Hill,
where the outside trees and the shrubs scattered generally through the
wood glow through the green, yellow, and scarlet, like fires
just kindled at the base of the trees, — a general conflagration just fairly
under way, soon to envelop every tree. The hillside forest is all aglow
along its edge and in all its cracks and fissures, and soon the
flames will leap upwards to the tops of the tallest trees.

October 4, 1859

How interesting now, by wall-sides and on open springy hillsides, the
large, straggling tufts of the dicksonia fern above the leaf-strewn
greensward, the cold, fall-green sward! They are unusually preserved about
the Corner Spring, considering the earliness of this year. Long, handsome
lanceolate green fronds, pointing in every direction, recurved and
full of fruit, intermixed with yellowish and sere brown and shriveled ones.
The whole clump, perchance, strewn with fallen and withered maple
leaves and overtopped by now withered and unnoticed osmundas.
Their lingering greenness is so much the more noticeable now that the
leaves (generally) have changed. They affect us as if they were evergreen,
such persistent life and greenness in the midst of their own decay. . . .
No matter how much withered they are, with withered leaves
that have fallen on them, moist and green they spire above them, not
fearing the frosts, fragile as they are. Their greenness so much the more
interesting because so many have already fallen and we know that the first
severer frost will cut off them too. In the summer greenness is cheap; now
it is something comparatively rare and is the emblem of life to us.

October 7, 1857

I saw, by a peculiar intention or dividing of the eye, a very striking
subaqueous rainbow-like phenomenon. . . . Those brilliant shrubs, which
were from three to a dozen feet in height, were all reflected,
dimly so far as the details of leaves, etc., were concerned, but brightly as
to color, and, of course, in the order in which they stood, —
scarlet, yellow, green, etc.; but, there being a slight ripple on the surface,
these reflections were not true to their height though true to their breadth,
but were extended downward with mathematical perpendicularity,
three or four times too far, forming sharp pyramids of the several colors,
gradually reduced to mere dusky points. The effect of this
prolongation of the reflection was a very pleasing softening and blending
of the colors, especially when a small bush of one bright tint stood
directly before another of a contrary and equally bright tint. It was just as
if you were to brush firmly aside with your hand or a brush a fresh line
of paint of various colors, or so many lumps of friable colored powders.

October 16, 1857

A great part of the pine-needles have just fallen. See the carpet of
pale-brown needles under this pine. How light it lies upon the grass, and
that great rock, and the wall, resting thick on its top and its shelves,
and on the bushes and underwood, hanging lightly! They are not yet flat
and reddish, but a more delicate pale brown, and lie up light as
joggle-sticks, just dropped. The ground is nearly concealed by them.
How beautifully they die, making cheerfully their annual contribution
to the soil! They fall to rise again; as if they knew that it was not
one annual deposit alone that made this rich mold in which
pine trees grow. They live in the soil whose fertility and bulk they
increase, and in the forests that spring from it.

I mark the summer's swift decline;
The springing sward its grave-clothes weaves.
Oh, could I catch the sounds remote!
Could I but tell to human ear
The strains which on the breezes float
And sing the requiem of the dying year!
                    — *Journal,* undated

October 10, 1858

The simplest and most lumpish fungus has a peculiar interest to us,
compared with a mere mass of earth, because it is so obviously organic
and related to ourselves, however remote. It is the expression of
an idea; growth according to a law; matter not dormant, not raw,
but inspired, appropriated by spirit. If I take up a handful of earth,
however separately interesting the particles may be, their relation to one
another appears to be that of mere juxtaposition generally.
I might have thrown them together thus. But the humblest fungus
betrays a life akin to our own. It is a successful poem in its kind.
There is suggested something superior to any particle of matter, in the
idea or mind which uses and arranges the particles.

October 17, 1858

Methinks the reflections are never purer and more distinct than now
at the season of the fall of the leaf, just before the cool twilight has come,
when the air has a finer grain. Just as our mental reflections are more
distinct at this season of the year, when the evenings grow cool and lengthen
and our winter evenings with their brighter fires may be said to begin.

November 1, 1855

This is the aspect under which the Musketaquid might be represented
at this season: a long, smooth lake, reflecting the bare willows and button
beeches, the stubble, and the wool-grass on its tussock, a muskrat-cabin
or two conspicuously on its margin amid the unsightly tops of pontederia,
and a bittern disappearing on undulating wing around a bend.

November 8, 1858

It is remarkable how little any but a lichenist will observe on the bark
of trees. The mass of men have but the vaguest and most indefinite notion
of mosses, as a sort of shreds and fringes, and the world in which the
lichenist dwells is much further from theirs than one side of this earth
from the other. They see bark as if they saw it not. . . .
Each phase of nature, while not invisible, is yet not too distinct and
obtrusive. It is there to be found when we look for it, but not demanding
our attention. It is like a silent but sympathizing companion in
whose company we retain most of the advantages of solitude,
with whom we can walk and talk, or be silent, naturally, without the
necessity of talking in a strain foreign to the place.
I know of but one or two persons with whom I can afford to walk.
With most the walk degenerates into a more vigorous use of your legs,
ludicrously purposeless, while you are discussing some mighty argument,
each one having his say, spoiling each other's day, worrying one
another with conversation. . . . I know of no use in the walking part
in this case, except that we may seem to be getting on together towards
some goal; but of course we keep our original distance all the way.
Jumping every wall and ditch with vigor in the vain hope of
shaking your companion off. Trying to kill two birds with one stone,
though they sit at opposite points of compass, to see nature
and do the honors to one who does not.

October 25, 1852

. . . Some small bushy white asters still survive.
The autumnal tints grow gradually darker and duller, but not less rich
to my eye. And now a hillside near the river exhibits the darkest,
crispy reds and browns of every hue, all agreeably blended.
At the foot, next the meadow, stands a front rank of smoke-like maples
bare of leaves, intermixed with yellow birches. Higher up, are red oaks
of various shades of dull red, with yellowish, perhaps black oaks
intermixed, and walnuts, now brown, and near the hilltop,
or rising above the rest, perhaps, a still yellow oak, and here and there
amid the rest or in the foreground on the meadow, dull ashy
salmon-colored white oaks large and small, all these contrasting
with the clear liquid, sempiternal green of pines.

July 25, 1851

It is the most perfect seashore I have seen. The rockweed falls
over you like the tresses of mermaids, and you see the propriety of that
epithet. You cannot swim among these weeds and pull yourself up
by them without thinking of mermen and mermaids.

November 25, 1850

The landscape looked singularly clean and pure and dry, the air,
like a pure glass, being laid over the picture, the trees so tidy, and stripped
of their leaves; the meadows and pastures, clothed with clean
dry grass, looked as if they had been swept; ice on the water and winter
in the air, but yet not a particle of snow on the ground. The woods,
divested in great part of their leaves, are being ventilated.
It is the season of perfect works, of hard, tough, ripe twigs, not of tender
buds and leaves. The leaves have made their wood, and a myriad
new withes stand up all around pointing to the sky, able to survive the
cold. It is only the perennial that you see, the iron age of the year.

WINTER

This afternoon, being on Fair Haven Hill, I heard the sound of a saw, and soon after from the Cliff saw two men sawing down a noble pine beneath, about forty rods off. . . the last of a dozen or more which were left when the forest was cut and for fifteen years have waved in solitary majesty over the sprout-land. I saw them like beavers or insects gnawing at the trunk of this noble tree, the diminutive manikins with their cross-cut saw which could scarcely span it. . . . I watch closely to see when it begins to move. Now the sawers stop, and with an axe open it a little on the side towards which it leans, that it may break the faster, and now their saw goes again. Now surely it is going; it is inclined one quarter of the quadrant, and, breathless, I expect its crashing fall. But no, I was mistaken; it has not moved an inch; it stands at the same angle as at first. It is fifteen minutes yet to its fall. Still its branches wave in the wind, as if it were destined to stand for a century, and the wind soughs through its needles as of yore; it is still a forest tree, the most majestic tree that waves over Musketaquid. The silvery sheen of sunlight is reflected from its needles; it still affords an inaccessable crotch for the squirrel's nest; not a lichen has forsaken its mast-like stem, its raking mast, — the hill is the hulk. Now, now's the moment! The manikins at its base are fleeing from their crime. They have dropped the guilty saw and axe. How slowly and majestically it starts! As if it were only swayed by a summer breeze, and would return without a sigh to its location in the air. And now it fans the hillside with its fall, and lies down to its bed in the valley, from which it is never to rise, as softly as a feather, folding its green mantle about it like a warrior, as if, tired of standing, it embraces the earth with silent joy, returning its elements to the dust again. But, hark! . . . You only saw, but did not hear. There now comes up a deafening crash to these rocks, advertising you that even trees do not die without a groan. . . . It is lumber. . . . When the fish hawk in the spring revisits the banks of the Muskatequid, he will circle in vain to find his accustomed perch, and the hen-hawk will mourn for the pines lofty enough to protect his brood. . . . I hear no knell tolled, I see no procession of mourners in the streets, or the woodland aisles. The squirrel has leaped to another tree; the hawk has circled farther off, and has now settled upon a new eyrie, but the woodman is preparing [to] lay his axe to the root of that also.

January 2, 1859

Going up the hill through Stow's young oak woodland, I listen
to the sharp, dry rustle of the withered oak leaves. This is the voice of
the wood now. It would be comparatively still and more dreary here in
other respects, if it were not for these leaves that hold on.
It sounds like the roar of the sea, and is enlivening and inspiriting like
that, suggesting how all the land is sea-coast to the aerial ocean.
It is the sound of the surf, the rut of an unseen ocean, billows of air
breaking on the forest like water on itself or on sand and rocks.
It rises and falls, wells and dies away, with agreeable alteration as the sea
surf does. Perhaps the landsman can foretell a storm by it. It is remarkable
how universal these grand murmurs are, these backgrounds of sound, —
the surf, the wind in the forest, waterfalls, etc., — which yet to
the ear and in their origin are essentially one voice, the earth-voice, the
breathing or snoring of the creature. The earth is our ship, and this is the
sound of the wind in her rigging as we sail. Just as the inhabitant of
Cape Cod hears the surf ever breaking on its shores, so we countrymen
hear this kindred surf on the leaves of the forest.

January 24, 1856

I have seen many a collection of stately elms which better deserved to be
represented at the General Court than the manikins beneath, —
than the barroom and victualling cellar and groceries they overshadowed.
When I see their magnificent domes, miles away in the horizon, over
intervening valleys and forests, they suggest a village, a community, there.
But, after all, it is a secondary consideration whether there are
human dwellings beneath them; these may have long since passed away.
I find that into my idea of the village has entered more of the elm than of
the human being. They are worth many a political borough.
They constitute a borough. The poor human representative of his party
sent out from beneath their shade will not suggest a tithe of the
dignity, the true nobleness and comprehensiveness of view, the
sturdiness and independence, and serene beneficence that they do.
They look from township to township. . . . They battle with the
tempests of a century. See what scars they bare, what limbs they lost
before we were born! Yet they never adjourn; they steadily vote for their
principles, and send their roots farther and wider from the same center.
They die at their posts, and they leave a tough butt for the choppers
to exercise themselves about, and a stump which serves for their
monument. They attend no caucus, they make no compromise, they use
no policy. Their one principle is growth. They combine a true
radicalism with a true conservatism. Their radicalism is not a cutting
away of roots, but an infinite multiplication and extension of them under
all surrounding institutions. They take a firmer hold on the earth that they
may rise higher into the heavens. . . . Their conservatism is a dead
but solid heart-wood, which is the pivot and firm column of support to all
this growth, appropriating nothing to itself, but forever by its support
assisting to extend the area of their radicalism. Half a century
after they are dead at the core, they are preserved by radical reforms.
They do not, like men, from radicals turn conservatives. Their
conservative part dies out first; their radical and growing part survives.
They acquire new States and Territories, while the old dominions decay,
and become the habitation of bears and owls and coons.

In the twilight I went through the swamp, and the yellow birches
sent forth a dull-yellow gleam which each time made my heart beat faster.
Occasionally you come to a dead and leaning white birch, beset
with large fungi like ears or little shelves, with a rounded edge above.
I walked with the yellow birch. The prinos is green within. If there were
Druids whose temples were the oak groves, my temple is the swamp.
Sometimes I was in doubt about a birch whose vest was
buttoned smooth and dark, till I came nearer and saw the yellow
gleaming through, or where a button was off.

March 9, 1852

Again it rains, and I turn about.
The sounds of water falling on rocks and of air falling on trees
are very much alike.
Though cloudy, the air excites me. Yesterday all was tight as a stricture
on my breast; to-day all is loosened. It is a different element
from what it was. The sides of the bushy hill where the snow is melted
look, through this air, as if I were under the influence of some
intoxicating liquor. The earth is not quite steady nor palpable
to my senses, a little idealized.

January 21, 1853

I wish to hear the silence of the night, for the silence is something
positive and to be heard. I cannot walk with my ears covered. I must
stand still and listen with open ears, far from the noises of the village,
that the night may make its impression on me. A fertile and eloquent
silence. Sometimes the silence is merely negative, an arid and
barren waste in which I shudder, where no ambrosia grows. I must hear
the whispering of a myriad voices. Silence alone is worthy to be heard.
Silence is of various depths and fertility, like soil. Now it is a mere
Sahara, where men perish of hunger and thirst, now a fertile
bottom, or prairie, of the West. As I leave the village, drawing nearer to
the woods, I listen from time to time to hear the hounds of
Silence baying the Moon, — to know if they are on the track of any game.
If there's no Diana in the night, what is it worth? . . . The
silence rings; it is musical and thrills me. A night in which the silence
was audible. I heard the unspeakable.

January 12, 1855

Perhaps what most moves us in winter is some reminiscence of
far-off summer. . . . What beauty in the running brooks! What life!
What society! The cold is merely superficial; it is summer still at the
core, far, far within. It is in the cawing of the crow, the crowing of the
cock, the warmth of the sun on our backs. I hear faintly the cawing
of a crow far, far away, echoing from some unseen wood-side,
as if deadened by the springlike vapor which the sun is drawing from
the ground. It mingles with the slight murmur of the village, the sound of
children at play, as one stream empties gently into another,
and the wild and tame are one. What a delicious sound! It is not merely
crow calling to crow, for it speaks to me too. I am part of one
great creature with him; if he has voice, I have ears. I can hear
when he calls, and have engaged not to shoot nor stone him
if he will caw to me each spring.

January 5, 1856

The thin snow now driving from the north and lodging on my coat
consists of those beautiful star crystals, . . . Nature is full of genius, full
of the divinity; so that not a snowflake escapes its fashioning hand.
. . . The same law that shapes the earth-star shapes the snow-star.
As surely as the petals of a flower are fixed, each of these countless
snow-stars comes whirling to earth, pronouncing thus, with emphasis, the
number six. Order, κοσμος. . . .
What a world we live in! where myriads of these little disks, so
beautiful to the most prying eye, are whirled down on every traveler's
coat, the observant and the unobservant, and on the restless squirrel's fur,
and on the far-stretching fields and forests, the wooded dells,
and the mountain-tops. Far, far away from the haunts of man, they roll
down some little slope, fall over and come to their bearings, and
melt or lose their beauty in the mass, ready anon to swell some little rill
with their contribution, and so, at last, the universal ocean from which
they came. There they lie, like the wreck of chariot-wheels after
a battle in the skies. Meanwhile the meadow mouse shoves them aside
in his gallery, the schoolboy casts them in his snowball, or the
woodman's sled glides smoothly over them, these glorious spangles,
the sweepings of heaven's floor. And they all sing, melting as they sing
of the mysteries of the number six, — six, six, six. He takes up
the waters of the sea in his hand, leaving the salt; He disperses it in
mist through the skies; He recollects and sprinkles it like grain in
six-rayed snowy stars over the earth, there to lie till
He dissolves its bonds again.

January 7, 1857

But alone in distant woods or fields, in unpretending sproutlands
or pastures tracked by rabbits, even in a bleak and, to most, cheerless day,
like this, when a villager would be thinking of his inn, I come to
myself, I once more feel myself grandly related, and that cold and
solitude are friends of mine. I suppose that this value, in my case,
is equivalent to what others get by church-going and prayer. I come to my
solitary woodland walk as the homesick go home. I thus dispose of
the superfluous and see things as they are, grand and beautiful.
I have told many that I walk every day about half the daylight, but I think
they do not believe it. I wish to get the Concord, the Massachusetts,
the America, out of my head and be sane a part of every day. . . .
I wish to forget, a considerable part of every day, all mean, narrow, trivial
men. . . . , and therfore I come out to these solitudes, where the
problem of existence is simplified. I get away a mile or two from the
town into the stillness and solitude of nature, with rocks, trees,
weeds, snow about me. I enter some glade in the woods, perchance, where
a few weeds and dry leaves alone lift themselves above the surface
of the snow, and it is as if I had come to an open window.
I see out and around myself. . . . This stillness, solitude, wildness of
nature is a kind of thoroughwort, or boneset, to my intellect.
This is what I go out to seek. It is as if I always met in those places
some grand, serene, immortal, infinitely encouraging, though
invisible, companion, and walked with him.

January 26, 1853

There are from time to time mornings, both in summer and in winter,
when especially the world seems to begin anew, beyond which
memory need not go, for not behind them is yesterday and
our past life; when, as in the morning of a hoar frost, there are visible
the effects as of a certain creative energy.
. . . The world has visibly been recreated in the night. Mornings of
creation, I call them. In the midst of these marks of a creative energy
recently active, while the sun is rising with more than usual splendor,
I look back . . . for the era of this creation, not into the night,
but to a dawn for which no man ever rose early enough. A morning which
carries us back beyond the Mosaic creation, where crystallizations are
fresh and unmelted. It is the poet's hour. Mornings when men
are new-born, men who have the seeds of life in them.